SUPERWOMAN

**SEASON 7,
LOS ANGELES**

Jessie Graff's second-place finish in L.A. made history, breaking her own record for highest finish by a woman in a city competition.

WORLD CHAMPION!

USA VS. WORLD

Rock climber and *Ninja* rookie Stefano Ghisolfi represented Europe well, becoming only the third competitor to crush Stage 3 on the course.

ENTER THE NINJAS

American Ninja Warrior has gone from fluke to phenomenon in less than a decade. Every year, athletes from all walks of life push themselves to the limit on the *Ninja Warrior* training course. Leaping, swinging and climbing their way through obstacles that test their resolve, the competitors seek not only Total Victory, but also to answer the question, "How far can I push myself?" That question, asked by viewers around the world, has made *American Ninja Warrior* the most vicarious and aspirational experience on TV. Fans gather in droves and tune in by the millions to cheer the winners, lament for the losers and wonder how they'd fare on the road to Mount Midoriyama. This ultimate guide looks at where *Ninja Warrior* came from, where it's going and showcases the athletes and challenges that make it great. Welcome to the future of sports. Are you ready for the challenge?

NOTHING IS OUT OF THIS NINJA'S GRASP!

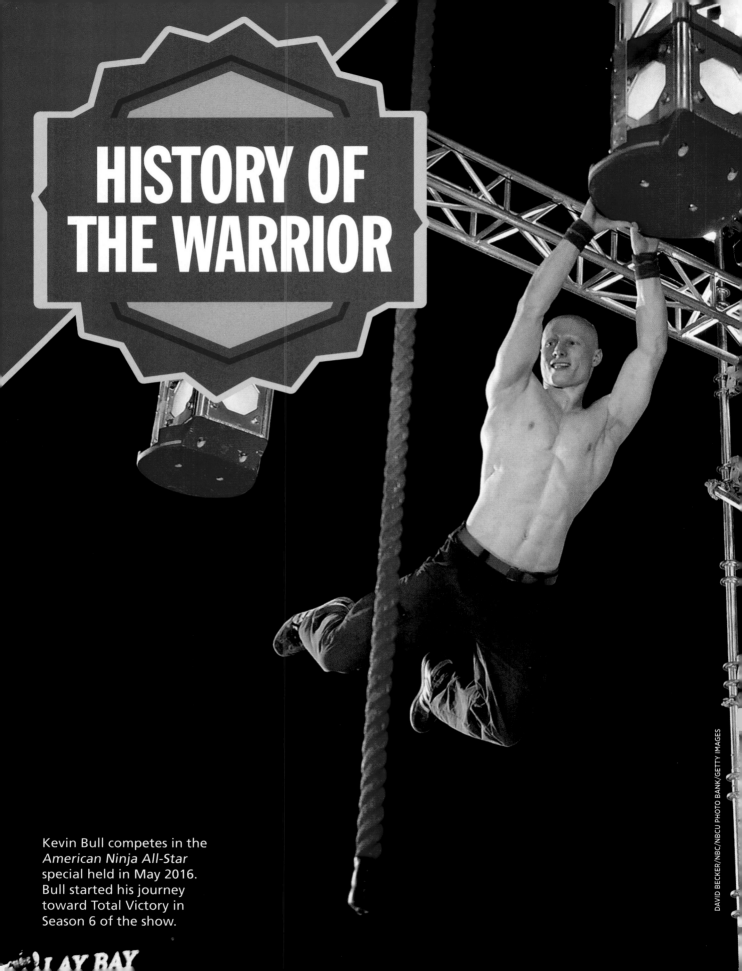

HISTORY OF THE WARRIOR

Kevin Bull competes in the *American Ninja All-Star* special held in May 2016. Bull started his journey toward Total Victory in Season 6 of the show.

SASUKE!

Nearly 20 years ago, a Japanese game show debuted that changed television, and quite possibly sports, for all time.

In Japanese lore, Sarutobi Sasuke is a ninja whose deeds have been written about since the 15th century. These stories celebrate his nimbleness, dexterity and monkey-like speed. Some stories have even claimed that the young hero was actually raised by monkeys. So when Japanese production company Monster 9 decided to create an obstacle course that would test the speed, strength and agility of competitors, it was only fitting that they dub the show *Sasuke*.

Sasuke had its origins as a segment on *Kinniku Banzuke*, a show comprised of a variety of physical challenges, ranging from walking on one's hands to navigating a course on stilts. The segment proved popular and, in 1997, the very first *Sasuke* hit the airwaves. The concept of the show was a simple one. ➡

Fleet of Foot
In feudal Japan, a child born into a ninjutsu family would begin training in childhood, which included exercises to improve agility. Those skills are tested with obstacles such as the log run.

SASUKE VS. NINJA WARRIOR

1 While *American Ninja Warrior* requires competitors to be 21 years or older, *Sasuke* places no limits on age or nationality.

2 The main focus of *Sasuke* is pitting the competitor against the course itself, whereas *American Ninja Warrior* adds another layer to the competition by having challengers face each other in qualifying rounds.

3 Each *Sasuke* installment is one contest in one three-hour episode. *American Ninja Warrior* lasts an entire season before reaching Mount Midoriyama.

Scaling New Heights
Ancient ninjutsu training involved hours of climbing, which is reflected in *Sasuke*'s Warped Wall obstacle.

MAKING THE IMPOSSIBLE POSSIBLE!

One hundred competitors worked their way through four obstacle course stages, each one designed to test them in a different way. The first course was a test of the competitor's athletic ability, Stage 2 was a test of speed, while Stage 3 allowed contestants to demonstrate their upper body strength. Those who actually made it to the final stage found themselves at the mercy of Sasuke Tower, a vertical climb whose height would increase every time someone conquered it. Those who made the climb could claim *kanzenseiha*, or "complete domination."

Right from the start, the show was a smash. From 1997 through 2011, 27 *Sasuke* tournaments were produced which led to a variety of spinoffs, including *Ninja Warrior UK*, *Swedish Ninja Warrior* and *Sasuke Vietnam*. But it was the journey to America, and the show's transformation into *American Ninja Warrior*

ILLUSTRATION BY NICK HARRAN: DAVID BECKER/NBC/NBCU PHOTO BANK/GETTY IMAGES

that made it a global sensation.

JOURNEY TO AMERICA

As *Sasuke* continued to grow in popularity, American TV took notice. In 2007, G4 began airing *American Ninja Challenge*, a competition show that featured contestants running a small obstacle course, with a select group of winners being offered the chance to compete on *Sasuke*. The show proved so popular that, in 2009, *American Ninja Warrior* was born.

The early seasons of the show took cues from other reality competitions of the time. Contestants, upon winning the qualifying rounds in Venice Beach, moved on to a "boot camp" of sorts, competing in *Survivor*-esque challenges for a shot at heading to Mount Midoriyama, Japan, and a chance at total victory. "The major difference between the two shows was that, in Japan, ninjas had to ➡

All-Stars
From left: Kenji Takahashi, Masashi Hioki, Yusuke Morimoto, Ryo Matachi and Tomo Kawaguchi comprise the Japanese team for the third season of *American Ninja Warrior: USA vs. the World.*

GOING GLOBAL

Sasuke has become an international blockbuster, with new editions of the show cropping up in various countries around the globe. Here are just a few examples of the world's other *Ninja Warrior* proving grounds.

DENMARK
DANMARKS
NINJA WARRIOR

SWEDEN
NINJA WARRIOR
SVERIGE

UNITED KINGDOM
NINJA WARRIOR
UK

UNITED STATES
AMERICAN
NINJA WARRIOR

TEAM NINJA
WARRIOR

TURKEY
NINJA WARRIOR
TURKIYE

FRANCE
NINJA WARRIOR:
LE PARCOURS
DES HÉROS !

SAUDI ARABIA
NINJA WARRIOR
BEL3ARABI

VIETNAM
KHÔNG GIỚI HẠN -
SASUKE VIỆT NAM

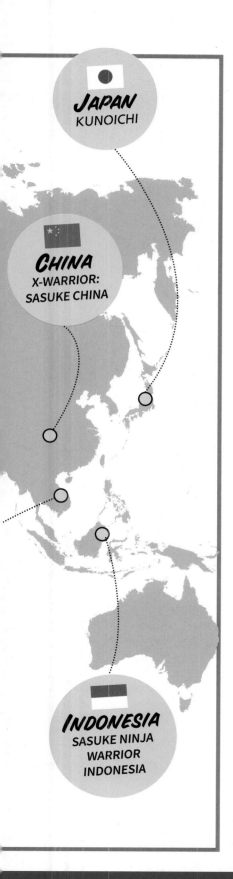

JAPAN
KUNOICHI

CHINA
X-WARRIOR:
SASUKE CHINA

INDONESIA
SASUKE NINJA
WARRIOR
INDONESIA

complete the course in a certain amount of time, and any or all—or none—of the 100 competitors could advance from Stage 1 to 2. In the American version, the top 30 advanced regardless of their speed," noted Spenser Mestel in *Rolling Stone*. "The courses were also slightly different. In *Sasuke*, Stage 2 was entirely new, while on the American course, obstacles were simply added to Stage 1."

After three successful years on the air, *Ninja Warrior* received an overhaul spurred on by the bankruptcy of Monster 9 and the folding of G4. After being picked up by NBC and Esquire TV, *American Ninja Warrior* was revamped into its current form. Gone were the boot camp challenges and the trips to Japan, with the new Mount Midoriyama being constructed in Las Vegas. "As a result," wrote Mestel, "the *Ninja* universe

greatly expanded. Competitors became more intense. It seemed like everyone and his brother (and his doctor and stepfather) was building a course replica in their backyard."

As *American Ninja Warrior* continued to grow, the show became a truly national sensation, with six cities around the country hosting qualifying rounds in 2015. In addition, *Ninja* fever doesn't die down when the lights dim on Mount Midoriyama. "Our best athletes train year-round for *ANW* now," producer Brian Richardson told *Mental Floss*. "There are gyms devoted to *Ninja* training that are popping up all over the country, so people have a lot more access to obstacles like the Warped Wall. We want to test them every year, so we have to keep creating obstacles that are fun, and challenging, and entertaining to watch at home."

FAST FACTS

The Log Grip obstacle, which requires Warriors to cling to a log for dear life as they're lowered to a platform, has been part of *ANW* since Season 3.

CHOSEN FOR GREATNESS

Think you have what it takes to achieve Total Victory? Here's what you need to know to get on the course and prove your _Ninja Warrior_ prowess.

At one time or another, everyone who watches _American Ninja Warrior_ asks themselves the same question: "I wonder if I could do that?" If you're an American resident over the age of 21, you may have a chance to prove it. "It's actually a pretty simple process," Season 7 finalist Geoff Britten told _The Washington Times_. "You have to fill out a very detailed questionnaire. It's, like, 20 pages long. Every question about [yourself] you ever wanted to answer, and you have to make a video. The video is very important. This year, it's a two-minute video. When I first started, it was a four-minute video about who you are and why you'd do [well] on the show. That's what they look at. The first season I did it, they had 5,000 people apply. Last season they had 50,000 people apply for 500 spots."

WALKING ON

If you aren't chosen based on your submission video, you can always try to get on the show as a walk-on contestant, which is how Isaac Caldiero landed his first *Ninja Warrior* gig, appearing at a Denver casting in a homemade Jesus costume. Of course, showing up as a walk-on is a grueling, days-long process in which the only guarantee is that you're going to wait in line for a long time. Make no mistake, participating at a walk-on is no promise that you'll be *Ninja Warrior* bound. "You sleep in a tent for a week or more outside the course, with no

guarantees," producer Brian Richardson said in an interview with *Mental Floss*. "We usually only have time to run 20 to 30 people from the walk-on line. Sometimes people spend a week camping out and never get to run the course."

If you're lucky enough to make it through the initial casting process, you may find yourself being invited by the producers to take your chances on the qualifying course and, if all goes well, ultimately find yourself on the road to Mount Midoriyama. ➡

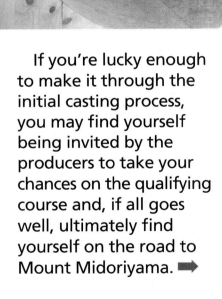

Tough Training
Donovan Schneider trains for greatness on a homemade version of the Warped Wall obstacle he constructed in his barn in Nebraska. Schneider competed in Indianapolis for Season 8 but could only complete three of six obstacles.

MODEL WARRIOR

While the path to Total Victory demands a tremendous amount of physical and mental conditioning, Warriors come in all shapes and sizes. One of the most inspiring stories to emerge from *American Ninja Warrior 8* was the performance of Artis Thompson III, a contestant with a prosthetic leg. Despite lacking a limb, ATIII made a run at the course, demonstrating the indomitable spirit of a true Warrior.

Ninja Strong
Staff Sgt. Randall Forsythe trains for his appearance on a special episode of *American Ninja Warrior* paying tribute to those serving in our military, which aired July 6, 2015. "I am always switching my workout routine up," Forsythe said in an interview with *Air Force Medicine*. "I guess the biggest thing is that I like to keep my body guessing."

THINK YOU CAN HANG WITH HIM?

MIND OVER MATTER

Regardless of your strength, agility or proven ability to rock the Salmon Ladder, at the end of the day, *American Ninja Warrior* is a TV show, and that means the producers are looking for people who will shine on-screen. "We look for people with big personalities and lots of good energy," Anthony Storm, an executive producer who also does casting for *American Ninja Warrior*, told *Bodybuilding*. "Of course we want people with the physical abilities to succeed on the obstacles, but we also want the audience to be drawn to the contestants."

Super Human
Reko Rivera doesn't always wear a cape. He took a run at the *American Ninja Warrior 8* Atlanta course dressed in a T-Rex costume and passed several obstacles before getting eliminated by the Spin Cycle.

PHILLY PRIDE

SEASON 8, PHILADELPHIA FINALS

In the City of Brotherly Love, native son Najee Richardson made his city proud, coming back from a knee injury that ended his gymnastics career to compete on *American Ninja Warrior*.

PATH
OF THE
WARRIOR

Competitor Nikko Galang watches his step at the Atlanta qualifer during Season 8. Although he gave it his all, Nikko did not claim Total Victory.

BUILDING GREATNESS

The ATS team creates the course that turns wannabes into Warriors.

Watching *American Ninja Warrior*, viewers can't help but wonder what kind of fiendish mind conceives of the various obstacles, devices and snares the competitors must navigate. But, instead of a laboratory full of evil masterminds, the people responsible are an outdoor training company from California.

Founded in 1999 by firefighter and rock climber Darren Jeffrey, Alpine Training Services (ATS) had its beginnings as an outdoor adventure company. The success of the programs ATS offered elevated the company's profile, and soon they were designing challenges for *American Ninja Warrior*.

Inside the *Ninja Warrior* compound (a sprawling warehouse covering 30,000 square feet) everything starts with an idea. Sketches, blueprints and scribblings of obstacles in various

Testing it Out
Nate Moore (left) and Kyle DesChamps test a course under construction in Kansas City, Missouri. ATS has also worked on challenges for *The Biggest Loser* and *The Amazing Race*.

stages of design litter the walls of the ATS Team's elaborate production house in Pacoima, California, which also includes a full metal shop, wood shop and paint studio. "Basically we're putting together a really large menu of obstacles," ATS project manager J.J. Getskow said in *American Ninja Warrior Nation*. "The producers go through them and say 'Like it, like it, love it, hate it.' From that stage we

Did You Know?

One of the rules of *American Ninja Warrior* is that you can't have the same obstacle in the same region, so the producers have to constantly keep track of which obstacles have been used where.

On a filming day, the ATS Team is constantly in motion, checking and rechecking everything on the course. Spyros Varnvas said that he walks 13–15 miles on an average night!

either do tweaks to it on paper, and once they say, 'Yes, let me see a demo of it,' then we go and [say] 'OK, how do we fabricate it?' "

The team works fast, building obstacles as quickly as they can be conceived and signed off on. "In like four days, you could go from light-bulb idea to prototype and then to actuality," said ATS COO Travis McDaniel. On the day

of filming, it's a constant cycle of safety tests and checks to ensure everything is working the way it's supposed to. "We go obstacle by obstacle by obstacle to make sure it's safe," said project manager Spyros Varnvas. "Make sure all the padding is in place. Make sure all the clamps are tight. Everything is a big old team collaboration; we all have to bring it together."

LEAP OF FAITH

SCOUTING VICTORY

SEASON 8, LOS ANGELES QUALIFIERS

Eagle Scout Jackson Meyer opted not to compete in his uniform on this night, as he'd done before. Perhaps he should have, as he fell short on the course, losing his grip on the I-Beam.

NINJA WARRIOR:
TOUGHEST
OBSTACLES

From the Jumping Spider to the Hourglass Drop to Bungee Road, a look at the most challenging obstacles Warriors must face and the best methods with which to defeat them.

SWING SPIKES

Not for the faint of heart, this obstacle requires Warriors to grasp spikes resembling nunchaku and swing to the next set, trusting in his or her skills to make it to the next end.

DISC RUNNER

Say what you will about this obstacle, but it lets you know what it is all about with its name. Leaping onto the first disc, competitors must hold on to a center pole, rotating themselves around until they reach the proper height to leap to the second disc. From there, it's an easy jump to the mat. Well, easy being a relative term. Time the jump wrong and the discs continue to spin, sending challengers flying into the water.

BETTER MOVE IT!

FLOATING BOARDS

A climbing obstacle, but one that also tests Warriors' balance and precision, the Floating Boards jut out from the wall above the water and force challengers to navigate over them using only their hands and feet to steady themselves. It's as difficult as it sounds and has shattered many a Ninja Warrior's dream of achieving Total Victory.

INVISIBLE LADDER

Replacing the Spider Climb as the final obstacle on the city courses, the Invisible Ladder requires Warriors to yank their way up a 30-foot chute by alternating tugs on a pair of suspended rings. Sounds easy enough, but after the strain of completing the previous obstacles, ascending the ladder has proven to be a more daunting challenge than most Warriors would have expected.

CIRCUIT BOARD

As much of a puzzle as it is an obstacle, navigating the Circuit Board requires you to slide a pair of handles through zig-zagging slots, then remove them precisely and reinsert them to continue the traverse. A test of brains as well as brawn, the Circuit Board has ended many a journey to Mount Midoriyama.

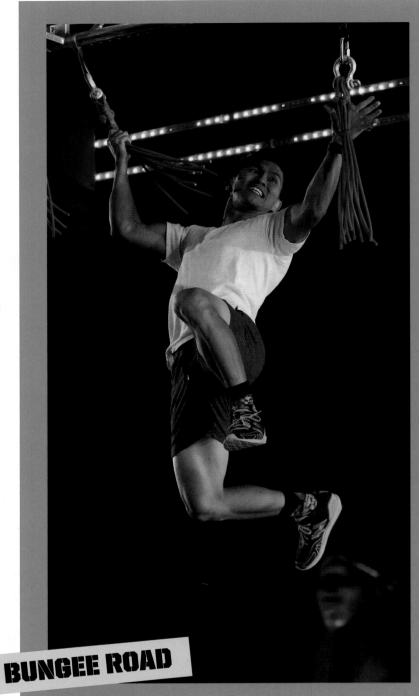

BUNGEE ROAD

Swinging Tarzan-like through a circuit of hanging bungee cords, contestants must work their way from one side to the other, then shimmy down a length of pipe before leaping to the mat. The catch? The bungees stretch with each grab, making the reach to the next rope that much more difficult. Strength and timing are your allies here.

JUMPING SPIDER

A *Sasuke* original and *Ninja Warrior* staple, this is consistently one of the toughest obstacles on the course, with nearly a quarter of competitors failing on each season it's appeared. Springing up from a trampoline, warriors must climb a chute simply by bracing their arms and legs against the wall. The Jumping Spider was the obstacle that ended Kacy Catanzaro's historic run in 2014 and, in Season 8, it even managed to take down Season 7 winner Isaac Caldiero!

THE ULTIMATE TEST OF STRENGTH AND SKILL

HOURGLASS DROP

One of *Ninja Warrior*'s most insane obstacles, the Hourglass Drop is a proven game-ender for a number of competitors. Contestants must shimmy their way along an hourglass-shaped shelf, then drop down to a trampoline, acquiring enough bounce to reach a second hourglass and then work their way to the landing. "It's sick, it's crazy," executive producer Kent Weed told *Entertainment Weekly*. "I would say the majority of our runners we lost on that one obstacle."

FLY WHEEL

This wicked device requires strength, timing and precision. Two wheels hang suspended over the water. Warriors must jump onto the first wheel, then swing back and forth, gaining momentum before leaping to the next wheel. The process is repeated and, if all goes well, they'll be launched safely onto the mat. If not, they'll simply end up in the water.

HOLLYWOOD HEIGHTS

**SEASON 8,
LOS ANGELES FINALS**
K.C. Halik came close to advancing to the next round but saw his dreams of Total Victory end after a failed I-Beam attempt.

THE WARPED WALL

Defeating the course's most challenging obstacle is an uphill battle, literally. And one that has seen the end of many a Ninja Warrior's path to Total Victory.

It looks deceptively easy on television. A steep ramp with a short runway, the famed Warped Wall seems like an obstacle that, compared to some of the others Ninja Warriors face on the road to Total Victory, would be a relative breeze. Not so. With a sharp curve that can extend as high as 14 ½ feet, the Warped Wall has brought the dreams of many a Warrior to a close. "It's like running up the side of a building and catching a window ledge on the second floor," explained Evan Dollard, who has competed in several *Ninja Warrior* competitions and hosts *Well Trained Warrior* on YouTube.

With only three attempts to make it, almost everyone who has faced the Wall has failed at least once. Some competitors have said it requires nothing more than commitment and the unshakable belief that you can do it. Others maintain that physics come into play, with speed, torque and velocity needing to be precisely measured in order to achieve success. Kacy Catanzaro, the first woman to beat the Warped Wall, made about 50 practice runs in the weeks leading up to her 2014 *Ninja Warrior* performance. "It's one of the toughest obstacles because there's such a specific technique," she told ESPN. "You have to adjust your speed upward—fast—to make it to the top. And it's scary! You feel like you are going to fall backward off of it."

1

EXPLOSIVE START!

The runup to the wall is all about generating horizontal velocity that will convert to enough vertical velocity to beat the wall.

esquire
NETWORK

AMERICAN
NINJA
WARRIOR
2015

19 FEET

Height of the "Mega Wall" version of the obstacle deployed at the end of *American Ninja Warrior: All-Star Special* in 2016.

3

PUSH TO VICTORY!

The last step on your run needs to be a combination of a verticle jump while also a push toward the wall. Hang on tight!

2

LEAN BACK!

According to some experts, as soon as you hit the wall you need to lean back and keep accelerating for success.

NO WALL CAN STOP A TRUE WARRIOR!

16'

Moravsky

SWINGING AWAY

SEASON 8, OKLAHOMA CITY FINALS
Hamidullah Khazi handled himself well on the Tire Swing, but it was the Bar Hop, an obstacle that ended a lot of bids for victory that night, that ended up cutting his run short.

THE SALMON LADDER

In *American Ninja Warrior*, they say only the strong survive. But when it comes to defeating this obstacle, strength isn't everything.

If *American Ninja Warrior* has a breakout obstacle, it's the Salmon Ladder. Not only is it a fixture on the course every year, but the acrobatic challenge has also become a fixture in pop culture. Such shows as *Arrow* and *The Flash* have both featured their titular heroes training on the ladder as they prepare to save the day.

Like the fish from which the obstacle takes its name, Ninja Warriors must call on their core to conquer the ladder. "You're exploding your body up, extending your arms so that you can reach the next rung and carrying your body weight up with your knees," J.J. Woods, a competitor in Season 7, explained to *Esquire*. Upper body strength is important but not essential. "I've had people walk into my gym who look like they were sculpted from marble, but they have no air awareness," Woods told *Esquire*. "Then I've had other guys come in who may not be much to look at, but they understand the mechanics of the body. So sure, there may be hope for you."

35

30

25

2 PUT A WIGGLE IN IT!

More important than even upper body strength is the ability to generate momentum with your core to keep you climbing those rungs!

4 STORIES TALL

The equivalent of what Mike Bernardo (pictured) scaled when he conquered all 35 rungs of the Super Salmon Ladder in 2016's *American Ninja Warrior All-Stars Skills Competition.*

1 PULL IT TOGETHER!

The most basic skill to master for the brutal climb is the simple pull-up. But that only gets you so far...

NBC

#FYC #AmericanNinjaWarrior

AmericanNinjaW

#FYC

NBC

STRIKE A POSE

LIVE EVENT, LOS ANGELES, CA
From left: Casey Suchocki, host Matt Iseman, Ben Malick and Thomas Stillings goof off before an *American Ninja Warrior* screening event at Universal Studios on August 24, 2016. Those in attendance didn't just get to watch the show—a live demonstration took place as well.

#FYC

NBC

THE BEST OF THE BEST

American Ninja Warrior has created some incredible, memorable and downright entertaining moments. Here are just a few that stand out from the rest.

RYAN STRATIS SHOWS MILITARY MIGHT

SEASON 8, PHILADELPHIA QUALIFIERS

A member of the National Guard, this military man has competed in every single season of *American Ninja Warrior*, but it was his performance in Season 8 that made him an immortal. After having shoulder surgery, Ryan was definitely not at 100 percent when he stepped on to the course in Philadelphia. But he pushed through the pain and managed to complete the course and even scaled the daunting Warped Wall!

JOHN LOOBEY PROVES AGE IS JUST A NUMBER

Season 8, Philadelphia Qualifiers

At 64 years old, this karate instructor from Bristol, Pennsylvania, became the oldest competitor ever to run the *Ninja Warrior* course. Although he didn't advance to the finals, Loobey did complete the course. Whether other senior citizens decide to toss aside their walkers for a try at the Jump Hang remains to be seen. But Loobey may prove to be a pioneer in a whole new demographic of Ninja Warriors.

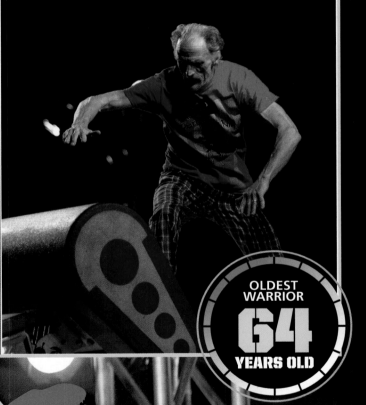

OLDEST WARRIOR

64

YEARS OLD

SAM SANN FIGHTS THROUGH INJURY

Season 5, Denver Qualifiers

After leaping from the Delta Bridge, Sann injured his leg, leading everyone watching to believe the gym owner from Houston, Texas, was done. However, Sann was not about to quit and stunned the crowd when he vaulted up the Warped Wall on the first try. The incredible feat was a reminder to everyone that physical toughness is only part of the formula for success in *Ninja Warrior*. It takes mental strength as well.

T-REX RUNS THE COURSE

Season 8, Atlanta Qualifiers

Was it a gimmick? A prank? Some kind of publicity stunt? No one is sure, but the fact remains that competitor Reko Rivera donned a T-Rex costume, stormed the course in Atlanta and actually managed to take down three obstacles! If there's an open call for the next *Jurassic Park* movie, someone should call this guy's agent.

KACY CATANZARO SHATTERS THE CEILING

SEASON 6, DALLAS FINALS

Before there was Jessie, there was Mighty Kacy, who made the *Ninja Warrior* record books when she became the first female competitor ever to complete a city finals course, leaping her way to the top in a seemingly effortless run. Although she came up short in later attempts, this unbelievable feat set a new standard for female competitors everywhere.

LEAPING INTO NINJA WARRIOR LEGEND

TOTAL VICTORY HAPPENS TWICE

SEASON 7, VEGAS FINALS

After a long drought in *American Ninja Warrior,* the world drank deeply in the Vegas Finals of Season 7 when not one but two competitors achieved Total Victory, becoming the first Ninja Warriors to conquer Mount Midoriyama. Geoff Britten was the first ever to accomplish this feat, but it was Isaac Caldiero who became the first true Ninja Warrior, beating Geoff's time by mere seconds. Isaac may have won the million that night, but both he and Geoff were a part of *Ninja Warrior* history.

VICTORY AT LAST!

FLIP RODRIGUEZ'S WATER LANDING

Season 6, Miami Qualifiers

David "Flip" Rodriguez is a standout *Ninja Warrior* competitor, having competed on both the *Sasuke* and *Ninja* courses. But his run almost came to a permanent end when, while on the Jump Hang, he skimmed the water just enough to result in a disqualification. So crushed was he that Flip considered never competing again. However, he eventually overcame his anguish and returned to compete in Seasons 7 and 8.

KEVIN BULL DEFEATS CANNONBALL ALLEY

Season 6, Venice Finals

No stranger to adversity, Kevin Bull was born with a rare form of alopecia, an autoimmune disorder that kills hair before it can grow. But he never let the disease shake his confidence, and his can-do attitude led to one of *Ninja Warrior*'s most unforgettable moments. During the Venice finals, Cannonball Alley had proven to be one of the most difficult challenges of the night. Bull decided to upend expectations by traversing the first two cannonballs with his arms and then swinging upside down and grabbing the last one with his feet. The unprecedented move made him a *Ninja Warrior* legend for all time.

JESSIE GRAFF WARPS EXPECTATIONS

SEASON 8, VEGAS FINALS

Jessie Graff had already won fans over with her superhero style, but she earned gasps and cheers when she became the first woman ever to complete Stage 1 in the national finals. Her run up the Warped Wall and one-handed grab at the top proved a spectacular finish to an incredible run. Fans were so enthused by Jessie's feat, they even crafted a LEGO version of her groundbreaking moment.

WAY OF THE WARRIOR

Jessie Graff swings into action during the *American Ninja All-Stars* competition. The stuntwoman remains one of the most impressive Warriors in the show's history.

MEET THE HOSTS

Akbar Gbaja-Biamila and Matt Iseman are responsible for calling all the action and drama on *Ninja Warrior*.

MATT ISEMAN

Before becoming a professional TV host, Matt Iseman was training to become a professional healer. Following a with-honors degree from Princeton and an M.D. from the Columbia College of Physicians and Surgeons, Matt suddenly gave up medicine during his residency for a career in Hollywood. "My heart just wasn't in it as much as I was hoping it would be or as much as I felt it should be," he told *Chi-Town Rising*. "I decided to take some time off to clear my mind and reevaluate what I wanted to do in life." He decided to take a year in Los Angeles and try his hand at stand-up comedy. That year has become two decades of performing onstage, in movies and on TV as the co-host of *American Ninja Warrior*. In 2002, he performed at the Winter Olympics in Salt Lake City and then began traveling around the world, entertaining troops in Kosovo, Afghanistan and Iraq. In 2010, he joined *American Ninja Warrior*, hosting six of the show's seven seasons. Iseman has expressed no regrets about his career path. "I was trying to discover my passion," he told *Chi-Town Rising*. "I ended up finding out that I just loved performing.... I love being in front of the camera, so rather than saving lives, I'm telling jokes and talking about ninjas. And I'm very happy with it."

FAST FACTS

Matt Iseman doesn't just announce American Ninja Warrior, he also actually attempted the course! During a fan event, Iseman decided to go for it, completing one and a half obstacles before dropping out.

AKBAR GBAJA-BIAMILA

Akbar Gbaja-Biamila knows a thing or two about competition, having spent five years on the gridiron as a defensive end and linebacker in the NFL. A star athlete at Los Angeles's Crenshaw High School, Gbaja-Biamila went on to San Diego State University and, in 2003, was selected by the Oakland Raiders as a free agent. After five years as a pro player, Gbaja-Biamila began a career in broadcasting, which he had prepared for even during his college years. "I loved it since I was a kid," he told *Assignment X*. "I just remember watching some of my favorite shows growing up, watching some of the local broadcasters, I would just think, 'I would love to do something like this.'"

Following stints on CBS Sports and the NFL Network, Gbaja-Biamila joined *American Ninja Warrior* in 2014, where he quickly became famous for his "Akbarisms," witty one-liners that reference a particular competitor's career or

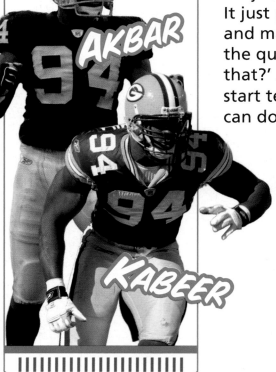

||||||||||||||||||||||
DID YOU KNOW?

Akbar's brother, Kabeer, was also a pro football player, spending nine seasons as a defensive end on the Green Bay Packers. The two brothers actually played each other when Akbar was on the Raiders!

AKBAR

KABEER
||||||||||||||||||||||

background. They've become popular enough to earn their own Twitter account (@ANWAkbarism). After three seasons working on the show, Gbaja-Biamila isn't surprised by its appeal. "Essentially, *American Ninja Warrior* is a sick and twisted version of some of your favorite childhood monkey bar experiences," he told *Cliche*. "You go to any park and you can see some sort of configuration that looks like an *American Ninja Warrior* obstacle. It just pokes at you and makes you ask the question, 'Can I do that?' And then you start telling yourself, 'I can do that.'"

FROM HOST TO HOST

Over the years, a number of TV personalities have helped bring you closer to the action on *American Ninja Warrior*.

Angela Sun

Angela was a sideline reporter for Season 4 and has gone on to direct a feature-length documentary, *Plastic Paradise*.

Jonny Moseley

A co-host for Season 4, Jonny is perhaps best remembered for winning gold in Mogul skiing at the 1998 Olympics in Nagano, Japan.

Jenn Brown

A sideline reporter for Seasons 5 and 6, Jenn is also an Emmy winner for her work as a sideline reporter on *Inside the NFL*.

Alison Haislip

After co-hosting the first season of *American Ninja Warrior*, Alison became a sideline reporter for Seasons 2 and 3.

Kristine Leahy

Kristine served as sideline reporter for the past two seasons, and can also be heard on Fox Sports Radio 1's *The Herd with Colin Cowherd*.

CALLING THE SHOTS LIKE NOBODY'S BUSINESS

CLIMB TO GLORY

SEASON 8, OKLAHOMA CITY
Amanda Smith, a rock climber from Fayetteville, West Virginia, was looking to go all the way but fell short on the Log Runner.

FATHER'S DAY

SEASON 7, PHILADELPHIA QUALIFIER
In *Ninja Warrior*'s seventh season, Jonathan Alexis Sr. and his son, Jonathan Alexis Jr., competed together, with both men making it to the finals in Las Vegas.

TRUE WARRIORS

Meet the men who conquered Mount Midoriyama and changed the face of *American Ninja Warrior* forever.

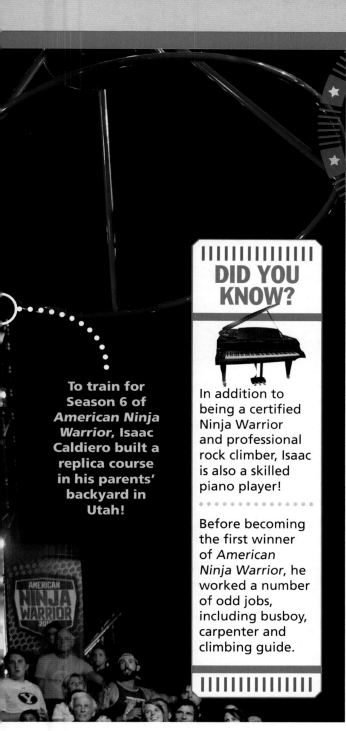

"YOU HAVE TO MAKE A TON OF SACRIFICES."

DID YOU KNOW?

In addition to being a certified Ninja Warrior and professional rock climber, Isaac is also a skilled piano player!

Before becoming the first winner of *American Ninja Warrior*, he worked a number of odd jobs, including busboy, carpenter and climbing guide.

To train for Season 6 of *American Ninja Warrior*, Isaac Caldiero built a replica course in his parents' backyard in Utah!

ISAAC CALDIERO

Before he was a millionaire and the first-ever winner of *American Ninja Warrior*, Isaac Caldiero's only focus was on the next climb. Since he was 17, Isaac has made rock climbing his living, working just enough to save for the next ascent. "Being a professional climber isn't glamorous," he said in an interview with *Forbes*. "There's not a lot of money in it, and you have to make a ton of sacrifices. At one point I was just eating cereal with water every day and sleeping in the back seat of my car to save money." Always eager for a challenge, Caldiero decided to try out for *Ninja Warrior*. He drove to Denver, where he attracted the attention of producers by donning a Jesus costume. After two failed attempts on the course, he approached year three with a calm, almost meditative state of mind, and it worked. On September 14, 2015, Caldiero completed the final course to achieve the famed Total Victory in 26.14 seconds, 3.24 seconds shorter than runner-up Geoff Britten, who also completed the course that night. Now, although he's a million dollars richer, Caldiero doesn't plan on changing much. "I want to go to all the amazing places I've never been," he told *Climbing*. "And just keep living this simple, frugal lifestyle that we've always lived. We have an old 1978 RV. We might put a new motor in it or something. But at the end of the day it's still: I just want to go rock climbing."

GEOFF BRITTEN

Growing up surfing in Hawaii, Geoff Britten was born to compete on *American Ninja Warrior*. But it was his wife who actually suggested he give the show a shot. Not long after, he made the jump to *American Ninja Warrior*, competing in Season 6 and making it to the finals before falling short on the Jumping Spider. In Season 7, he came back stronger, completing all six courses in the competition. In the finals, Geoff completed the course in Las Vegas, becoming the first competitor in *American Ninja Warrior* ever to achieve Total Victory. Unfortunately for Geoff, Isaac Caldiero beat his time by a mere 3.24 seconds to officially be crowned the first-ever *American Ninja Warrior*.

FAST FACTS

Although he wasn't the winner, Geoff had a perfect season in Season 7 by completing all six courses and hitting all six buzzers.

Did You Know?

At 36, Geoff is the oldest competitor to achieve Total Victory on *American Ninja Warrior.*

Geoff's unusually large forearms have earned him the nickname "Popeye."

When not competing on *American Ninja Warrior,* Geoff is a professional cameraman, running the video cameras in Washington D.C.'s Nationals Park and filming college football. He's also done work at the Olympics!

Geoff's wife, Jessica, is also an aspiring Ninja Warrior, having submitted a tape for Season 7.

COWBOY STYLE

Lance Pekus goes by the nickname "Cowboy Ninja," a nod to his other career as a ranch hand. Lance showed true grit on All-Stars, shimmying up the rope alongside Flip Rodriguez in the final climb but coming up just short of the win.

STRIKE A POSE

SEPTEMBER 18, 2016
Ninja Warrior's legendary lady Jessie Graff arrives at the Emmy Awards in Los Angeles. The show was nominated for Outstanding Reality Competition Program but lost out to *The Voice*.

WOMEN WARRIORS

In the history of *American Ninja Warrior*, many incredible female competitors have emerged to stand toe-to-toe with the men. Here are some of the fiercest ladies ever to attempt Mt. Midoriyama.

KACY CATANZARO

At just 5 feet tall, this Glen Ridge, New Jersey, native might not seem the most formidable, but on the *American Ninja Warrior* course, she is a force of nature. Exploding onto the scene in 2014, Kacy entered the *ANW* record books as the first woman to complete a qualifying course when she crushed the Warped Wall in Dallas. She continued her historic run to become the only woman to date to successfully complete a City Finals course. Kacy made it all the way to National Finals in Vegas before falling on the Jumping Spider. Kacy's determined to reclaim her glory and also wants to educate all the aspiring would-be Warriors out there. "I obviously have a huge passion for fitness, specifically for obstacles," she told *Esquire*, "so I want to continue to do that and inspire people." ➡

MICHELLE WARNKY

Hailing from Columbus, Ohio, Michelle became only the second woman to conquer the Warped Wall and made it on the wild card to the Vegas finals three years in a row. A devout Christian who has competed with inspirational verses written on her body, Michelle enjoys upending people's expectations of what a woman can do. "I grew up playing football, baseball, basketball, etc., with the guys in our neighborhood and always tried to keep up with my brother and others," she said in an online interview with Cameron Airen, "so it is fun to continue that type of lifestyle and compete alongside the men of *American Ninja Warrior.*"

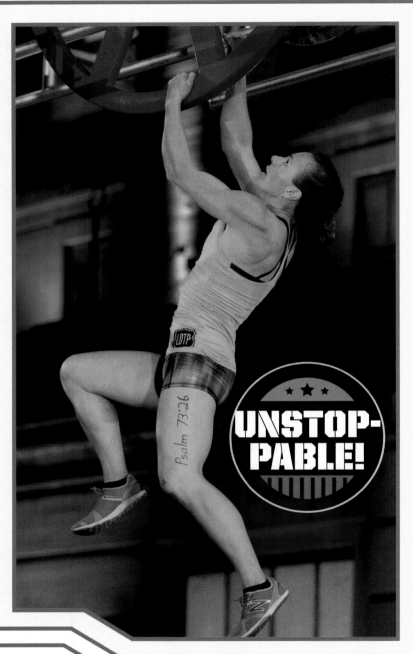

UNSTOP-PABLE!

NIKA MUCKELROY

Although she's only competed in two *Ninja Warrior* seasons, Nika has a place in the show's lore for being the first female competitor to make it to the sixth obstacle on a qualifying course in Denver. The following year, she was a favorite to go all the way and complete the qualifying course, but the Tilting Table proved to be her undoing. Time will tell if Nika decides to take on the course for a third time.

MEAGAN MARTIN

A climber from Boulder, Colorado, and three-time Ninja Warrior, Meagan made it to Vegas on her own (without a wild card invite), becoming only the third woman (after Kacy Catanzaro and Jessie Graff) to do so. Although she didn't complete Stage 1, her example still served as an inspiration for fierce females everywhere. "It means so much to me to be a role model," Meagan told ESPN. "I'm the oldest of three girls, so I think I've always made decisions with setting a good example in mind. Now with *American Ninja Warrior*, I am on a much bigger stage, so it's great to have the opportunity to show girls that they can be and do anything they put their mind to."

READY TO CRUSH HER NEXT CHALLENGE!

JESSIE GRAFF

A Hollywood stuntwoman by trade, Jessie Graff doubles for the titular Supergirl on the hit CW series. On the *American Ninja Warrior* course, she performed some super feats of her own. In Season 5, she was the first woman ever to compete in a City Finals course, even though she didn't complete it. But it was in Season 8 that Jessie went from stuntwoman to sensation. In the qualifying rounds in Los Angeles, she became the first woman to ever make it up the 14 ½-foot Warped Wall. Then, a few weeks later in Vegas, Jessie made history a second time as the first woman to complete Stage 1, finishing the course with 12 seconds to spare. The incredible achievement set social media alight and inspired countless tributes, including video of the moment rendered completely in LEGO. "As far as being the first woman to do it," she told ESPN, "there are more women than ever who are fully capable of doing what I did, and even more. I'm grateful that it came together for me on the right night, and I'm looking forward to seeing more women hit that buzzer in the future."

REACH FOR IT!

NAVAL WARFARE

MILITARY QUALIFIERS, SAN PEDRO, CA
A Naval officer known as "The Destroyer," Deon Graham fell on the I-Beam Cross, but his speed and distance were still enough to keep him in the running.

TRAINING LIKE A WARRIOR

To conquer the course, you need to turn your body into an obstacle-crushing machine. Here's how these Ninja Warriors prepared themselves for domination.

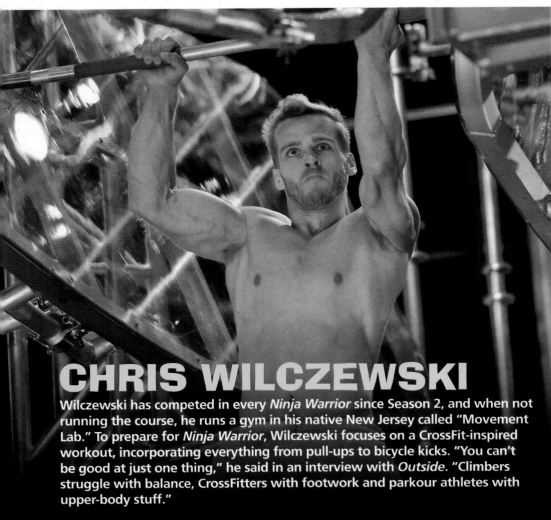

CHRIS WILCZEWSKI

Wilczewski has competed in every *Ninja Warrior* since Season 2, and when not running the course, he runs a gym in his native New Jersey called "Movement Lab." To prepare for *Ninja Warrior*, Wilczewski focuses on a CrossFit-inspired workout, incorporating everything from pull-ups to bicycle kicks. "You can't be good at just one thing," he said in an interview with *Outside*. "Climbers struggle with balance, CrossFitters with footwork and parkour athletes with upper-body stuff."

ISAAC CALDIERO

The first-ever *American Ninja Warrior* winner kickstarts his day with a glass of lukewarm water and lemon to wake up his body, then focuses on a workout that emphasizes cardio and pull-ups, along with a heavy dose of climbing. During the runup to his *Ninja Warrior* victory, Caldiero pushed his body to the limit. "I had these atomic climbing holds that you can dangle from a tree limb or a bar," he told *Outside*. "They build your grip strength well."

JAMES McGRATH

Nicknamed "The Beast," McGrath was a four-time finalist and competed in *American Ninja Warrior: USA vs. Japan*. When training to achieve Total Victory, McGrath's regimen included 100–300 pull-ups a day, workouts on a makeshift Salmon Ladder (part of a homemade obstacle course he constructed in his yard), hanging from his fingertips and scaling a 55-foot rope he has hanging from a tree. His training is focused on speed and agility, with the goal being to stay quick and avoid falling. "I get nervous about falling in general," he told the *Seattle Times*. "Falling means you failed. That's why I train this way."

BUILT TO WIN

JESSIE GRAFF

This stuntwoman turns to basic strength and conditioning to keep her body humming. Her program includes a sick overhand pull-up regimen, hanging intervals on a rock climbing fingerboard and dumbbell curls. But she also likes to change up her workouts when things get dull. She enjoys a variety of unusual workouts, including flying trapeze and, as she explained to *Byrdie*, "Anti-gravity yoga classes. You're in circus-like hammocks holding yoga poses which is great for learning air-awareness."

SHOWING SPIRIT

SEASON 8, PHILADELPHIA QUALIFIERS

By day, Jake Cahill works in the wine and spirits industry in his native Brooklyn. By night, however, his dreams were of *Ninja Warrior* glory. Sadly, his bid for Mt. Midoriyama was cut short in Philly.

THE WARRIOR'S

Over the last decade, *American Ninja Warrior* has gone from novelty to national sensation. And its momentum only seems to be growing.

BASKING IN THE WARM GLOW OF VICTORY

FUTURE

Making History
It was a legendary night in Las Vegas when Isaac Caldiero became the first-ever winner of *American Ninja Warrior*, completing the course just seconds less than Geoff Britten, who had gone immediately before.

When it debuted in the summer of 2007, *American Ninja Warrior* was kind of a curiosity, with muscular men running through an oversized jungle gym trying desperately not to fall in the water. But it didn't take long for the country to catch *Ninja* fever, and today the show draws nearly seven million viewers each week, not to mention throngs of hopeful competitors, who show up in droves at tryouts around the country. So the question is, what's the draw?

Part of the appeal is the fact that, for seven years, no one had achieved Total Victory, making every season a game of "Will they or won't they" for the viewer. Of course, there's no fear that viewership will ebb now that someone has reached the summit of Mt. Midoriyama. On the contrary, everyone is waiting to see if Isaac Caldiero was the exception, or the new rule.

For *Ninja Warrior* fans looking to get their fix, there will be plenty of chances going forward. "It is indeed built for TV—but also for phones and devices. (Lately, the producers have been experimenting with virtual reality.)," wrote Jason Gay in the *Wall Street Journal*. "It has the enormous benefit of editing itself down to its most exciting parts—something no baseball game or any other live sport can do." Spectators happy with the thrills they're enjoying now have only seen the tip of the iceberg.

AWARD CONTENDERS

AUGUST 24, 2016
In celebration of *American Ninja Warrior*'s first Emmy nomination, a special course demonstration was set up on the lot at Universal Studios. The course was constructed right in front of the courthouse from the 1985 film *Back to the Future*.

PEGGED FOR GREATNESS

AMERICAN NINJA WARRIOR ALL-STARS, 2016
Brian Arnold made a dominant display in the 2016 All-Stars special, crushing the competition and becoming the All-Stars champion.

This book is not endorsed by American Ninja Warrior or NBC Universal. The American Ninja Warrior Phenomenon is an unauthorized/unofficial guide.

ISBN-10: 1-942556-72-1
ISBN-13: 978-1-942556-72-5

Media Lab Books
For inquiries, call 646-838-6637

Copyright 2016 Topix Media Lab

Published by Topix Media Lab
14 Wall Street, Suite 4B
New York, NY 10005

Printed in the U.S.A.